MW01156337

Wisdom

...solve to be thyself

...ho finds himse...

and know that...

...loses his...

Wisdom

ARIEL BOOKS

**Andrews McMeel
Publishing**

Kansas City

For information write Andrews McMeel Publishing,
an Andrews McMeel Universal company,
4520 Main Street, Kansas City,
Missouri 64111.

Illustrations © 2001 Lyn Bishop
Edited by Margaret Lannamann

ISBN: 0-7407-1956-4
Library of Congress Catalog Card Number:
2001086410

Wisdom

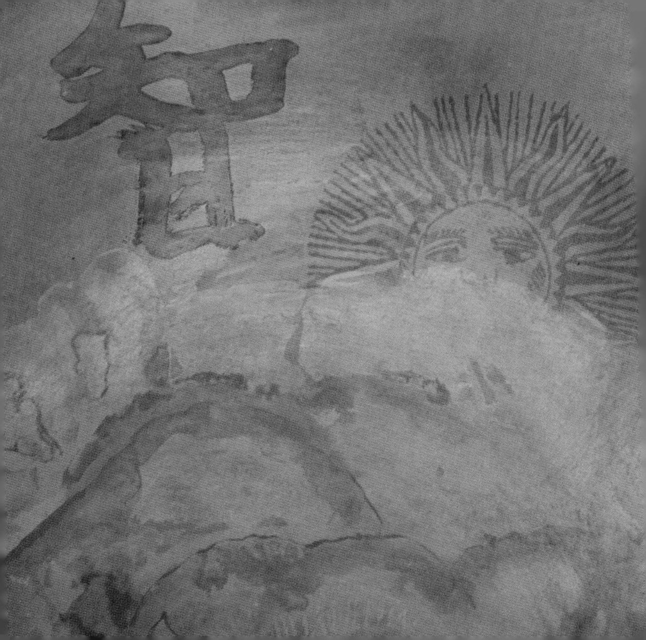

I AM PRESENT

TO THOSE WHO CONTEMPLATE ME;

I AM FOUND

AMONG THOSE WHO SEEK ME.

—Gnostic Gospel:
Nag Hammadi Library

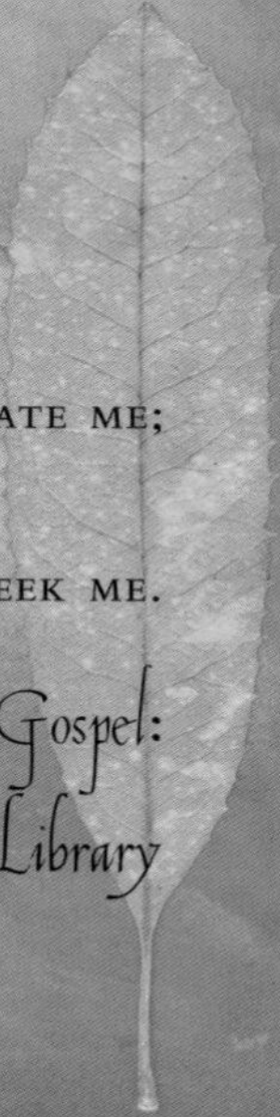

Wisdom...

BETTER THAN SWEET HONEY,

GATHERS MORE GLADNESS

THAN EVEN WINE,

ENLIGHTENS

MORE THAN THE SUN,

... PRICELESS ABOVE

FINE JEWELS ...

—Makeda, Queen of Sheba

Joy takes far away from us
the thoughts of our actions;
sorrow it is that awakens the soul.

—MARGUERITE OF VALOIS

AN INFINITE NUMBER OF THINGS.

'TIS THE ANSWER TO WHAT? AND HOW?

AND WHY?

AND WHENCE? AND WHITHER?

—A WORD WHEREBY

THE TRUTH (WITH THE COMFORT IT BRINGS)

IS OPEN TO ALL WHO GROPE IN NIGHT,

CRYING FOR WISDOM'S HOLY LIGHT.

—Ambrose Bierce

. . . to dry one's eyes and

laugh at a fall,

And, baffled, get up and

begin again . . .

—ROBERT BROWNING

Each soul

must meet the morning sun,

the new, sweet earth, and

the Great Silence alone!

—OHIYESA

LOOK

within!

The secret is inside you!

—HUI NENG

Sad soul,

take comfort, nor forget
that sunrise never failed us yet.

—CELIA LAIGHTON THAXTER

Non tener pur
ad un loco
la mente.

The fear of the Lord is
the beginning of
Wisdom.

—PSALM 111:10

You, seeker after knowledge,

look for the Oneness within.

—HADEWIJCH OF ANTWERP

Strengthen yourself
with contentment,
for it is an impregnable fortress.

—EPICTETUS

I have the greatest of all riches:
that of not desiring them.

—ELEONORA DUSE

Manifest plainness,

embrace simplicity,

reduce selfishness,

have few DESIRES.

—Lao-tzu

I try to teach my heart to want
nothing it can't have.

—ALICE WALKER

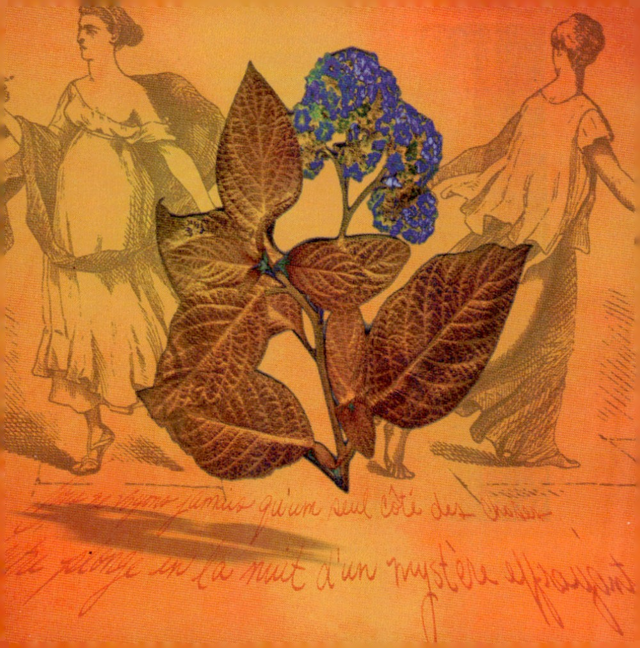
jamais qu'un seul côté des
plonge en la nuit d'un mystère effrayant

To be able to dispense with good things
is tantamount to possessing them.

—JEAN-FRANÇOIS REGNARD

BESIDES THE NOBLE ART OF

GETTING THINGS DONE,

THERE IS THE NOBLE ART OF

LEAVING THINGS UNDONE.

THE WISDOM OF LIFE CONSISTS IN

THE ELIMINATION OF NONESSENTIALS.

—Lin Yü-t'ang

I am erecting a barrier of simplicity
between myself and the world.

—ANDRÉ GIDE

I believe a leaf of grass is no less than
the journeywork of the stars.

—WALT WHITMAN

Speak to the earth,

and it shall teach thee.

—JOB 12:8

Whatever you can lose

. . . reckon of no account.

—PUBLILIUS SYRUS

No bird SOARS too high,

if he soars with his own wings.

—WILLIAM BLAKE

WE COULD NEVER LEARN TO BE

BRAVE AND PATIENT,

IF THERE WERE ONLY

JOY IN THE WORLD.

—Helen Keller

Si no temo perder
lo que poseo,
ni deseo tener
lo que no gozo,
poco de la Fortuna
en mí el destrozo
valdrá ...

I have often regretted my speech,

never my silence.

—PUBLILIUS SYRUS

ONE MUST BE CHARY OF WORDS

BECAUSE THEY TURN INTO CAGES.

—Viola Spolin

They

have sown the wind,

and they shall reap the

whirlwind.

—HOSEA 8:7

A word once let out of the cage
cannot be whistled back again.

—HORACE

Silence

is a true friend
who never betrays.

—CONFUCIUS

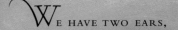

WE HAVE TWO EARS,

BUT ONLY ONE MOUTH,

SO THAT WE MAY LISTEN MORE

AND TALK LESS.

—Zeno of Elea

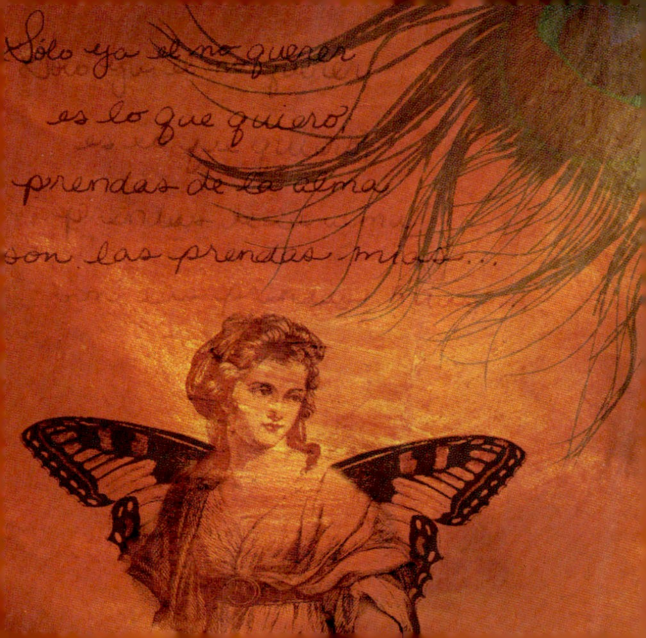
Sólo ya el no querer
es lo que quiero
prendas de la alma
son las prendas mías...

The bird that sweetest sings

can least endure the STORM.

—MARIA BROOKS

RESIGN YOUR BODY TO FATE

AND PUT UP WITH PAIN,

BECAUSE WHAT THE PEN

HAS WRITTEN FOR YOU

IT WILL NOT UNWRITE.

—Omar Khayyam

But pleasures

are like poppies spread,

You seize the flow'r,

its bloom is shed.

—ROBERT BURNS

THE WELL-INSTRUCTED **MOON**

FLIES NOT FROM HER ORBIT

TO SEIZE ON THE GLORIES

OF HER PARTNER.

—Margaret Fuller

Knowledge comes,

but wisdom lingers . . .

—ALFRED, LORD TENNYSON

The fox knows many things,

but the hedgehog knows

one great thing.

—ARCHILOCHUS

LISTEN TO MY SOFT VOICE

AND ALSO MY HARSH ONE.

I AM SHE WHO IS VOCAL,

I AM SCATTERED ABOUT

ON THE GROUND.

MY BREAD AND MY MIND

ARE RISING WITHIN.

MY NAME IS TRUTH.

—Gnostic Gospel:
Nag Hammadi Library

Believe nothing,

no matter where you read it,

or who said it,

no matter if I have said it,

unless it agrees with

your own reason and

your own common sense.

—Buddha

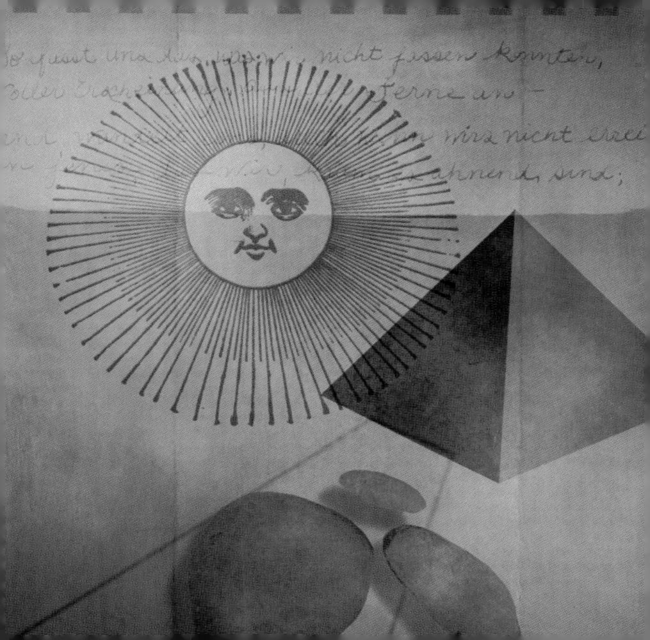
nicht fassen konnten,
Ferne un–
wird nicht
ahnend, sind;

"But the Emperor has nothing on at all!" said a little child.

—HANS CHRISTIAN ANDERSEN

CHOOSE ALWAYS THE **WAY**

THAT SEEMS THE BEST,

HOWEVER ROUGH IT MAY BE;

CUSTOM WILL SOON RENDER IT EASY

AND **AGREEABLE**.

—PYTHAGORAS

THERE IS ONE THING ALONE

THAT STANDS THE BRUNT OF LIFE

THROUGHOUT ITS COURSE:

A QUIET CONSCIENCE.

—*Euripides*

In spite of all the learned have said,
I still my opinion keep . . .

—PHILIP FRENEAU

Each man

the architect of his own fate.

—APPIUS CAECUS

Please all,

and you will please none.

—AESOP

listen to my soft voice
and also my hair on
... she who is locale ...
... scattered ...
on the ground ...
... bend ... wind
are rising ...
my name is ...

Knowledge

IS PROUD

THAT HE HAS LEARNED SO MUCH;

Wisdom

IS HUMBLE

THAT HE KNOWS NO MORE.

—William Cowper

THIS MUCH I KNOW:

LEARN FROM OTHERS

THEIR MULTITUDE

OF SKILLS.

—Bacchylides

A PERSON WHO DOESN'T KNOW
BUT KNOWS THAT HE DOESN'T KNOW
IS A STUDENT; TEACH HIM.
A PERSON WHO KNOWS BUT WHO
DOESN'T KNOW THAT HE KNOWS
IS ASLEEP; AWAKEN HIM.
BUT A PERSON WHO KNOWS
AND KNOWS THAT HE KNOWS IS WISE;
FOLLOW HIM.

—Asian proverb

...*Fire* CAN BE SEEN

IN YOUNG MEN'S EYES,

BUT IN THE OLD MAN'S EYES

THERE IS *Light*.

—Victor Hugo

To my extreme mortification,

I grow wiser every day.

—LADY MARY WORTLEY MONTAGU

If a beard, friend,

means wisdom,

even a goat

can pass for Plato.

—LUCIAN OF SAMOSATA

stra apprensiva da esser verace

ggel ... nzione, e dentro a lei la spi

chè l'animo ad essa volger face...

A little fool soon commits great foolishness.

—MARCABRU

It is only with the heart

that one can see rightly;

what is essential

is invisible to the eye.

—Antoine de Saint-Exupéry

The Truth

must dazzle gradually

Or every man be blind—

—EMILY DICKINSON

No man

was ever wise

by chance.

—SENECA

THE MAN

WHO NEVER ALTERS HIS OPINION

IS LIKE STANDING WATER,

AND BREEDS REPTILES OF THE MIND.

—William Blake

Happy

is he who is a bit mad,

and who, in his madness,

pleases himself and others!

—PIETRO ARETINO

voix à l'esprit parle dans son silence
n'a pas entendu cette voix dans son c

There are those who would misteach us that to stick in a rut is consistency—and a virtue, and that to climb out of the rut is inconsistency—and a vice.

—Mark Twain

Until you know that

LIFE is interesting

—and find it so—

you haven't found your **SOUL**.

—ARCHBISHOP GEOFFREY FISHER

He that is of a merry heart

hath a continual feast.

—PROVERBS 15:15

Stretch out your hand
and take the world's wide gift

OF

Joy and Beauty.

—CORINNE ROOSEVELT ROBINSON

Be cheerful while you are alive.

—PTAHHOTEP

We know accurately
only when we know little;
with knowledge doubt increases.

—JOHANN WOLFGANG VON GOETHE

demanderais; Et ce assez d'arracher
uez de Venise un soir, par aventure
re au fond de l'âme
une larme, et de partir
on baise ailleurs, sans

Three things
that come without asking:
fear, jealousy, love.

—SCOTS GAELIC TRIAD

The **WORLD** is too much with us;

late and soon

Getting and spending,

we lay waste our **POWERS**.

—WILLIAM WORDSWORTH

The unendurable . . .

the beginning of the curve of

JOY.

—DJUNA BARNES

One is forever
throwing away substance for shadows.

—JENNIE JEROME CHURCHILL

Zum ... wirds ihm, will es einer

Bestechen und trifft den, der

Ihm gleichen will mit Gewalt,

Pt überraschet es einen,

Der eben kaum es gedacht hat.

Don't wish me happiness—

I don't expect to be happy. . . .

wish me courage and strength

and a sense of humor—

I will need them all.

—Anne Morrow Lindbergh

I count life just a stuff
To try the soul's strength on.

—ROBERT BROWNING

A WOUNDED DEER—

LEAPS HIGHEST—

I'VE HEARD THE HUNTER TELL . . .

—Emily Dickinson

Wisdom

at times is found

in FOLLY.

—HORACE

Nowadays

most people die of a sort

of creeping common sense,

and discover when it is too late

that the only things one never

regrets are one's mistakes.

—Oscar Wilde

For all the blessed souls in heaven
Are both forgivers and forgiven.

—ALFRED, LORD TENNYSON

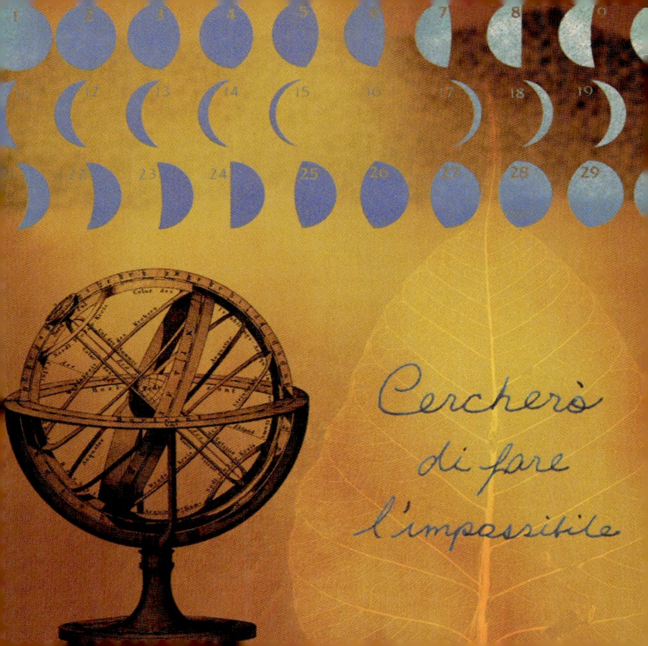
Cercherò
di fare
l'impossibile

The price of *Wisdom* is above rubies.

—JOB 28:18

Pain had a joy,

for suffering could but wring

Love from my soul.

—MARIA BROOKS

Believe one
who has tried it.

—VIRGIL

STRANGE WE NEVER PRIZE THE MUSIC

TILL THE SWEET-VOICED BIRD

HAS FLOWN.

—May Riley Smith

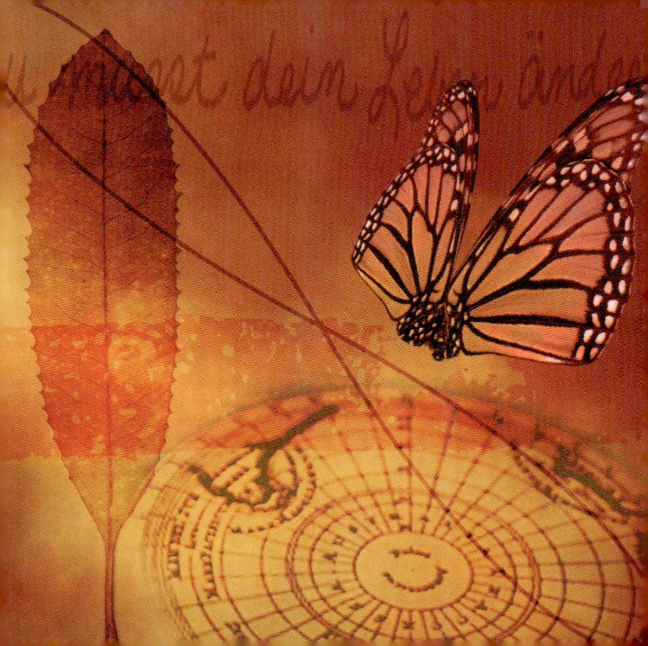
dein Leben

Losing an illusion
makes you wiser than finding a truth.

—LUDWIG BÖRNE

Deep WITHIN US,

A FIELD LIES FALLOW;

TEAR OUT ITS WEEDS

AND PLANT FLOWERS

OF Wisdom.

—Nguyên Binh Khiêm

It is not the answer that enlightens,
but the question.

—EUGÈNE IONESCO

You will find rest from vanities

if you go about every act in life

as though it were your last.

—*Marcus Aurelius*

The man who trusts other men
will make fewer mistakes than he
who distrusts them.

—CAMILLO DI CAVOUR

It is not enough to be wise,
          one must be engaging.

—NINON DE LENCLOS

Hear

the other side.

—ROMAN LAW PRINCIPLE

ACT ONLY ON THAT PRINCIPLE

WHEREBY YOU CAN AT THE SAME TIME

WANT THAT IT SHOULD BECOME

A UNIVERSAL LAW.

—Immanuel Kant

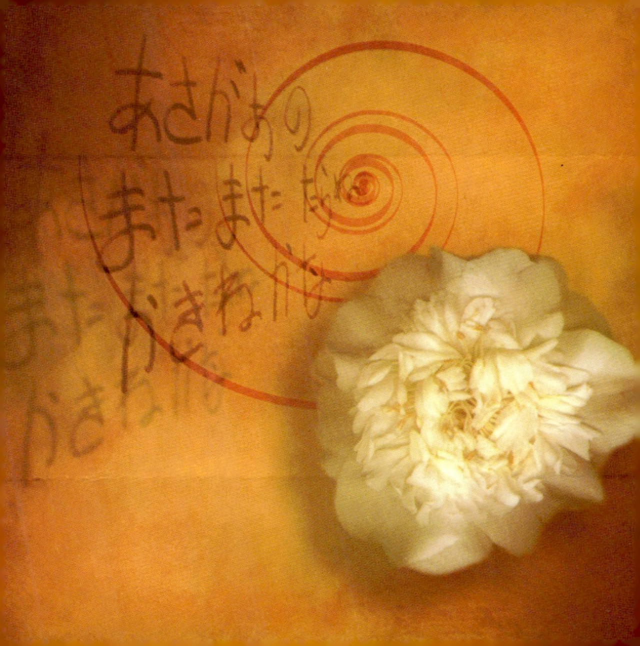
あさがおの

He who desires the fruit,
waters the tree.

—NGUYÊN TRÃI

Fools and the wise

 are equally harmless.

it is the half-fools

 and the half-wise

 that are dangerous.

—Johann Wolfgang von Goethe

A MAN SHOULD NEVER BE ASHAMED
TO OWN HE HAS BEEN IN THE WRONG,
WHICH IS BUT SAYING, IN OTHER WORDS,
THAT HE IS WISER TODAY
THAN HE WAS YESTERDAY.

—Alexander Pope

The clearest sign of **wisdom**

. . . continued cheerfulness.

—MICHEL DE MONTAIGNE

Believe one
who has
tried it

Notes

Aesop (c. 550 B.C.)

Alfred, Lord Tennyson (1809–1892), "Locksley Hall" (p. 43)

Andersen, Hans Christian (1805–1875), *The Emperor's New Clothes*

Archilochus (760–670 B.C.)

Aretino, Pietro (1492–1557), Letter to Count Manfredo di Collalto, thanking him for a gift of thrushes

Aurelius, Marcus (121–180)

Bacchylides (5th century B.C.)

Barnes, Djuna, *Nightwood*, 1937

Bierce, Ambrose (1842–1914), "Abracadabra"

Blake, William (1757–1827), *The Marriage of Heaven and Hell*

Börne, Ludwig (1786–1837)

Brooks, Maria (1795–1845), "Grove of Acadias," 1825

Browning, Robert (1812–1889), *In a Balcony* (p. 82); *Life in a Love* (p. 11)

Buddha (c. 563–483 B.C.)

Burns, Robert (1759–1796), "Tam O'Shanter"

Caecus, Appius (4th century B.C.)

Cavour, Camillo di (1810–1861)

Churchill, Jennie Jerome (1854–1921), Letter to her sister,
     Leonie Leslie, 1914

Confucius (551–479 B.C.)

Cowper, William (1731–1800)

Dickinson, Emily (1830–1886), "165" (p. 83); "1129" (p. 64)

Duse, Eleonora (1858–1924)

Epictetus (c. 55 B.C.–c. A.D. 135)

Euripides (c. 484–406 B.C.), *Hippolytus*

Fisher, Archbishop Geoffrey (1887–1972)

Freneau, Philip (1752–1832), "The Indian Burying Ground,"
     1788

Fuller, Margaret (1810–1850), "The Great Lawsuit. Man
     Versus Men, Woman Versus Women," 1843

Gide, André (1869–1951)

Gnostic Gospel: Nag Hammadi Library (2nd–4th century),
     "The Thunder: Perfect Mind"

Goethe, Johann Wolfgang von (1749–1832)
Hadewijch of Antwerp (13th century)
Horace (65–8 B.C.)
Hugo, Victor (1802–1885), *Booz Endormi*
Hui Neng (638–713)
Ionesco, Eugène (1912–1994)
Kant, Immanuel (1724–1804)
Keller, Helen (1880–1968), *Atlantic Monthly,* 1890
Khayyam, Omar (1048–1131), The Rubaiyat
Lao-tzu (c. 604-531 B.C.), *The Way of Life*
Lenclos, Ninon de (1620–1705)
Lin Yü-t'ang (1895–1976)
Lindbergh, Anne Morrow (1906–2001)
Lucian of Samosata (dates unknown), "Meditation on Beavers"
Makeda, Queen of Sheba (c. 1000 B.C.)
Marcabru (12th century)
Marguerite of Valois (1553–1615), *Memoirs*
Montagu, Lady Mary Wortley (1689–1762)
Montaigne, Michel de (1533–1592)

Nguyên Binh Khiêm (dates unknown), "On reading the Buddha's scriptures"
Nguyên Trãi (dates unknown)
Ohiyesa (1858–1939)
Pope, Alexander (1688–1744)
Ptahhotep (c. 2400 B.C.)
Pythagoras (c. 580–500 B.C.)
Regnard, Jean-François (1655–1709)
Robinson, Corinne Roosevelt (1861–1933), "Stretch Out Your Hand," 1912
Saint-Exupéry, Antoine de (1900–1944), *The Little Prince*
Seneca (1st century)
Smith, May Riley (1842–1927), "If We Knew," 1867
Spolin, Viola (c. 1911–)
Syrus, Publilius (1st century B.C.), Maxim 191 (p. 28); Maxim 1070 (p. 32)
Thaxter, Celia Laighton (1835–1894), "The Sunrise Never Failed Us Yet"
Twain, Mark (1835–1910)
Virgil (70–19 B.C.)

Walker, Alice (1944–), *The Color Purple,* 1982
Whitman, Walt (1819–1892), "Song of Myself," *Leaves of Grass,* 1855–1892
Wilde, Oscar (1854–1900)
Wordsworth, William (1770–1850), "The World Is Too Much with Us"
Zeno of Elea (c. 490–c. 420 B.C.)

Art Direction and Design
by BTDnyc

❧

This book is set
in Bembo and Tagliente.